Six Small Chicks

by Carolyn Kelly
illustrated by Pat Barbee

Hide and seek. You can't see us.
We are still in these six eggs.

Mom is a big hen.
She must sit on her eggs for
three whole weeks.

It is time for us to hatch.
We chip, chip, chip on the
white shells.

Look! We are free!
We are six small chicks.
We are balls of nice soft fluff.

We see mom peck at seeds.
We'll peck at seeds too.
Yum! Yum! Yum!

We look at Mom while she sips.
We sip. We like this stuff.

Time has passed.
We don't look the same now.
But aren't we cute?

Target Phonics Skills

CVCe
cute
hide
like
nice
same
these
time
while
white
whole

Long e: e, ee
free
see
seeds
seek
three
we
weeks

Digraphs sh, wh, th, ch, tch
chicks
chip
hatch
she
shells
the
these
this
while
white

Vowel Sound /o/ (a)
balls
small

Contractions
aren't
can't
don't
we'll

Unit 3 High-Frequency Words
her
now
too

UNIT 3

PEARSON

Scott Foresman

scottforesman.com

ISBN 0-328-21399-3

90000

9 780328 213993

Level A3